Girl in a Funk

Quick Stress Busters

(and why they work)

Tanya Napier and Jen Kollmer

Illustrated by Ali Douglass

ZEST BOOKS

First published in 2007 by
Zest Books, an imprint of Orange Avenue Publishing
35 Stillman Street, Suite 121, San Francisco, CA 94107
www.zestbooks.net

Created and produced by Zest Books, San Francisco, CA
© 2007 by Orange Avenue Publishing LLC
Illustrations © 2007 by Ali Douglass

Text set in Hoefler Text; title text set in Retrofit; accent text set in Rockwell

Library of Congress Control Number: 2007925699
ISBN-13: 978-0-9772660-9-8
ISBN-10: 0-9772660-9-5

CREDITS
EDITORIAL DIRECTOR: Karen Macklin
CREATIVE DIRECTOR: Hallie Warshaw
WRITERS: Tanya Napier and Jen Kollmer
EDITOR: Karen Macklin
ILLUSTRATOR: Ali Douglass
GRAPHIC DESIGNER: Cari McLaughlin
PRODUCTION ARTIST: Cari McLaughlin

Printed in China.
First printing, 2007
10 9 8 7 6 5 4 3 2 1

*Every effort has been made to ensure that the information presented is accurate. Readers are strongly
advised to read product labels, follow manufacturers' instructions, and heed warnings. The publisher
disclaims any liability for injuries, losses, untoward results, or any other damages that may result
from the use of the information in this book.*

Girl in a Funk

It's your usual Monday.

You were up all night trucking through a mountain of homework, your mom is on your case about dirty laundry or something, and now you're about to be late to school. You already know that today is going to suck. And, in general, you can't escape the sense that everything you do right now could be messing up your life. Forever.

There's no doubt about it, girl. You're stressed.

But what exactly does that mean? Stress is how your body reacts to surprises and disappointments in your life. It's a chemical reaction that happens in your body that can make you feel exhausted and worn out or frazzled and edgy—and not in a cool, rock-star sort

of way. Have you ever worried so much about a test, you couldn't think straight when you tried to study? Or been so mad, you snapped at anyone who came near you? Anger, frustration, sadness, fatigue, insomnia, and lack of appetite (or too much appetite!)—it's all related to stress.

But there's good news. While you can't control your teacher's lack of compassion when he comments on your essays or your mom's yelling when she finds wet towels on the floor, you can control how you *react* to what's going on and find ways to diffuse your stress. From self-acupressure to aromatherapy to fun psychological tricks, *Girl in a Funk* gives you tons of quick and easy stress remedies. And, so you can understand what's really happening in your mind and body, we also tell you why these solutions work.

When you feel the pressure piling up, use these tips to take the edge off. If you're tired or frustrated or totally lethargic, there's something inside that can help.

Including quick mellow-out tips,

and do-it-yourself spa treatments,

Girl in a Funk shows you how to get back to your calm and grounded self—and stay there.

Count Down your Anger

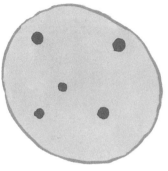

What's Going On

Just as the homeroom bell rings, your "best friend" lets it slip that she's going to the dance with the guy she knows you're in love with. You want to explode, but your teacher has zero tolerance for talking during morning announcements.

What to Do About It

Count to 10 before responding, taking a deep breath between each number. If deep breathing's out of the question, try using the phrase "chocolate chip cookie dough" between each number: one chocolate chip cookie dough, two chocolate chip cookie dough, and so on.

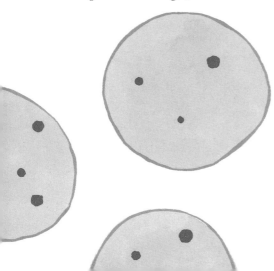

Why It Works

Taking your time gives you a chance to get it together before you say anything. When you are furious, you often say things you regret later on—you can minimize the damage by taking the 10-count first.

Have a Good Cry

What's Going On

While online one night doing research for an impossible paper, you notice that your boyfriend has announced on his blog that he's in love with another girl from the drama club. Tears start welling up in your eyes.

What to Do About It

Go for it. Have that cry. Flop down on your bed with a box of Kleenex and let it all out. You can even feed the weeping with a tearjerker like *A Walk to Remember* or *Romeo + Juliet* from the video store.

Why It Works

Studies show that most women feel better after crying. Why? It's a good emotional release. In fact, some scientists say that tears contain stress hormones and crying gets them out of your body. For each tear you cry, imagine that a problem gets washed away. Now with some of the negativity out of your system, you can finish your paper—and start looking for a new boyfriend.

Turn It Off

Do you check email every five minutes? Do you sleep with your cell phone plugged in, turned on, and tucked under your pillow? If you answered yes to any of these questions, it's time to unplug.

For one night, declare your room a technology-free zone: no Internet, no TV, no cell phone (there's such a thing as an off switch, you know). Hunker down with a book you've been meaning to read or a creative project you've wanted to work on. Constant technological interruptions and information overload prevent us from focusing on anything and keep our nerves on edge; letting it go for an evening will help you return to your natural state of calmness.

13

Don't Fight—Write

What's Going On

Permission to go out Saturday night? Denied. Latest English quiz? Flunked. Summer vacation? Canceled. Mood? Pissed.

What to Do About It

Sometimes the best way to let off a little steam is to write it out. Grab a piece of paper and spend 20 minutes writing about what's going on. Don't worry about spelling or grammar, just write anything that comes to mind. Keep going until the 20 minutes are up, even if that means using the same words over and over until something else comes to mind.

Why It Works

Novelists call this "free writing," but it can help "free" anyone from a bad mood. Studies have shown that writing about stressful events can help relieve the stress because getting it out on paper helps get it out of your brain.

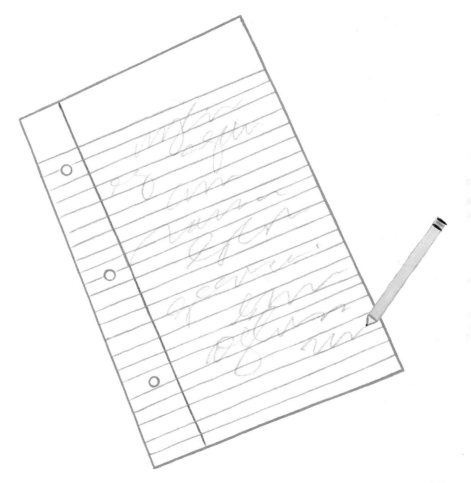

Laugh It Off

What's Going On

Nobody warns you about the massive patch of ice right in front of the school entrance, so of course you bite it. Spectacularly. And naturally this happens in full view of the crowd standing by. Nothing feels broken, but the laughter is so loud your eardrums and your ego hurt as much as your butt.

What to Do About It

Laugh with them. Before you get mad, give yourself a chance to see the humor in the situation. Then laugh about it as you get ready to tell your best friend the story of the Great Wipeout.

Why It Works

Laughing along not only eases the humiliation (you go instantly from being laughed *at* to laughing *with*), but it also actually lowers the levels of stress hormones and increases natural feel-good chemicals in your body. And you'll need those when you start feeling the massive bruise on your butt.

Go for a Soak

Cranky? Can't sleep? It's time for a classic stress reducer: the long soak in a hot tub. For an even more relaxing time, make it a chamomile tea bath. Here's the recipe:

1. Boil 4 chamomile tea bags, 5–7 sprigs of lavender, 4 tablespoons honey, and 4 cups of water on the stove (or in the microwave).

2. Let the mixture steep for a few hours.

3. Draw a warm bath. Add to the water 4 cups of fresh milk and the liquid from the steeped chamomile mixture (use a strainer to remove the solid bits).

4. Soak and enjoy!

Nap It in the Bud

What's Going On

In half an hour, you've got to head out for movie night with the girls, but this afternoon's softball practice has left you pooped. You can barely keep your eyes open now—how are you going to make it through that romantic comedy?

What to Do About It

Try a power nap. In big cities like New York and Tokyo, people shell out serious cash for 20 minutes in a "nap pod," but you can get the same effect in your own bed for free. Put on some relaxing music, set your alarm to go off in 20 minutes, and tell your siblings not to bug you. Then just crash out.

Why It Works

Studies show that 20 minutes of sleep in the afternoon gives you more rest than 20 minutes of extra sleep in the morning. (And you thought the snooze bar was good for you?) The trick is that when you sleep for just a short spell, you never enter a deep sleep, called REM sleep, when vivid dreams occur. So coming out of sleep is easier, and you wake up refreshed, instead of sleepier.

Abolish Stressful Finger Cramps

What's Going On

The paper's due first thing in the morning. You've got great ideas for your revision, but how far will you get if your hands feel like they're about to fall off?

What to Do About It

These stretches will give your typing fingers (plus your arms and shoulders) a break, so you can tackle that concluding paragraph:

1. Bend and straighten your fingers several times.

2. Hold your arms in front of you and clench your fists. Slowly curl your wrists inward, then back five times. Next, rotate your fists in circles.

3. Straighten your arms against your sides and press in for five seconds, then release them. Repeat this two or three times.

4. Keep your arms down and raise your shoulders toward your ears. Hold them up while you count to five, then let them drop back down. Repeat this one more time.

Why It Works

Stretching amps up the blood flow to your fingers, arms, and shoulders and helps keep your muscles loose. And taking a break before jumping into that bibliography is also a necessity for keeping sane.

Paws for Thought

There's a reason we love our pets so much. Quality time with Rex and Whiskers can totally chill you out. Studies have shown that caring for pets—or even watching fish swim around—lowers your blood pressure, increases your brain's feel-good chemicals, and cuts down on stress hormones. So, next time you are wigging out, take Fido for a jog or call Morris over for some belly scratching. If you don't have a pet of your own, snuggle up to your best friend's pup or kitty, or visit the local pet store for your furry fix. You can even pop in to a zoo or an aquarium and just watch the fish.

Overwhelmed? Break It Down

What's Going On

It's the lunch period that ruined your life. You spilled ketchup all over your favorite shirt, got into a major fight with your friend when she laughed at you, and in your rattled state dropped your math homework in a huge puddle. It's just too much to deal with.

What to Do About It

Though each one of these things is annoying, you're going to stand a much better chance of fixing them if you tackle them one at a time. Pick one problem—the one that's bothering you the most, or the first one you think of— and concentrate on it for a few minutes until you've got a solution. Then move on to the next one.

Why It Works

Deciding which problem to focus on is a subtle way to remind yourself that you are in control. This should get you past that overwhelming feeling of helplessness that was keeping you from thinking straight in the first place.

Refuel With Exercise

What's Going On

The dirty dishes are piling up on your nightstand again. It's gross, but you are too wiped out to peel yourself off the bed to wash them.

What to Do About It

When you find yourself lacking the energy you need to get through the day, squeeze in some exercise. If you have a hard time sticking to an exercise schedule on your own, work out with a friend or sign up for an aerobics class or a team sport that has lots of practices.

Why It Works

Even though it seems like exercise would make you more tired (and it might if you do it only once a year), working out regularly gives you way more energy. Plus, studies have shown that people who exercise aren't just in better shape, they're happier and less stressed, too. Exercise decreases levels of cortisol, the stress hormone. It also turns up your body's production of serotonin and endorphins, and that lifts your mood. Buff biceps will also come in handy when you finally get around to cleaning your room.

There's the Rub

There's nothing like the first week of softball season. The thrilling crack of the bat sending one into left field, the satisfying smack of the ball landing in your glove, the aching throb of your shoulders after practice.

If your body's feeling beat, you can banish stiff muscles with a soothing natural body rub. To make it, peel and mash a ripe banana and a ripe avocado together in a bowl. Use your hands to mash and get the mixture as smooth as possible. Then add a drop of eucalyptus essential oil and mix some more. When your mix is ready, spread out a beach towel, put on a bathing suit top, and rub it into your aching shoulders.

Stretch out on the towel and relax for 15 minutes before hitting the shower.

While avocados and bananas make a great creamy base, the eucalyptus oil contains a chemical that naturally reduces inflammation and pain. After a good rub, you'll be back on the field in no time.

Fake It Till You Make It

What's Going On

Moving to a new school sounded like a fun adventure when your parents brought it up last year, but your first day's "journey" is straight off the Titanic. You can't find your homeroom, and the sea of strangers in the hallway makes you want to hide under a desk.

What to Do About It

Even though you don't feel like it, it's time to show the biggest smile you can manage.

Why It Works

The saying "Fake it till you make it" is about more than getting through a tough time. Smiling through a nerve-wracking situation not only makes you look friendly and cool (which helps when you're a stranger in a strange land), but it actually lifts your mood. That's because smiling sends a signal to your brain that tells it to be calm. When your brain is calm, it'll send a signal to your mouth to keep smiling.

Tear It Up

Sometimes you need to get fired up before you can calm down. The next time the tension's mounting and you're in need of a fast way to get some angst out of your system, try this.

Take a piece of paper and write down your worries and fears. Get as elaborate as you want. When you've written everything down, take a deep breath and shred the paper—and your fears—into tiny bits. Doesn't that feel better?

Rate Your Worries

What's Going On

You have no idea what to wear to the big party on Saturday, never mind how to do your hair for yearbook pictures tomorrow. And then there's that oral presentation you have to give tomorrow in Spanish class. The only word you can remember is *pánico*.

What to Do About It

Using a scale of 1 to 10, with 1 being totally minor and 10 being a real catastrophe, assign a number to whatever's making you anxious. Think it through before you pick the number. How bad is it really? What is the worst thing that could happen? Have you been able to work through problems like this before?

Why It Works

Just because a problem feels like a 9 or a 10 at first, that doesn't mean it's a life-altering issue. When you look at each problem, you'll find that most of your day-to-day stress comes from smaller things that you already know how to handle.

About Face

After your third friend asks, "What's wrong?" you realize your lousy day is completely showing—on your face.

To loosen up your facial muscles, and your mood, try this self-massage:

1. Wiggle your face around. Raise and lower your eyebrows, puff out your cheeks, and relax your jaw.

2. Massage your ears by pulling gently on your earlobes and rubbing them.

3. Finish up with an easy stretch for your neck. Close your eyes and let your head slowly fall

forward. Slowly roll your head to the right and then to the left without pulling or straining.

4. Lift your head, open your eyes, and you're ready to face the rest of your day. And if you feel like a freak pulling on your ears in public, just sneak off to a corner where no one can see you.

39

Fight Stage Fright

What's Going On

The good news: You have your first role—as Emily in *Our Town*. The bad news: You completely forgot your lines and barely fudged your way through your first scene. Now you've got about 60 seconds to recuperate before going back out there.

What to Do About It

Use a personal mantra to refocus. This works not only backstage, but also in other stressful situations in which you need to regain composure.

First, you need to come up with a short phrase that works for you. Some mantras are religious or spiritual, and others are more secular. Whichever way you go, keep it simple and positive. Here are some possibilities to get you started:

"It's OK."   "Hail Mary."

"Let it be."   "Shalom."

"Om."   "Allah."

Once you've thought of a word or phrase you'd like to try, repeat it 10 times in your head, concentrating on the words. If you're alone, you can even whisper or say the words out loud.

Why It Works

Repeating a mantra helps you concentrate on something positive and important to you, giving your mind a chance to let go of whatever's stressing you out. Best of all, mantras are free, and nobody needs to know you're using one.

Brush Your Way to Bed

What's Going On

Night after night it's the same thing: You're sleepy and heading for bed, but as soon as you hit the sheets, your mind starts going a mile a minute.

What to Do About It

Have a look at your toothpaste. Before going to bed, try a calming, herbal blend instead of the usual supercharged flavor.

Why It Works

If you're brushing those teeth at night with something super minty, the extra zing in your paste may be jolting you awake right when you want to be lulled to sleep. Peppermint is great for staying alert, but that's not necessarily what you need when you're trying to sleep. Herbal toothpastes that have cinnamon, fennel, or lavender flavors—and less sugar—reduce the chance of stimulation before bedtime.

De-Stress With Yoga

Yoga is a spiritual tradition from India. Part of this tradition is doing *asanas*, postures that involve strength training and stretching.

One reason that yoga postures are so good for you is that, like all forms of exercise, they lower stress levels. Asanas also demand mental focus, which keeps your mind from being stressed and scattered.

Different asanas are good for different emotional states; forward bends (touching your toes) help relieve anxiety, while back bends are good for boosting energy when you're in a slump. It's best to learn with a trained instructor. Try a yoga class at a local YMCA, gym, or studio. If you can't find anything in your area and budget range, you can follow a DVD or download yoga videos from the Internet.

45

Light Up Your Life

What's Going On

During winter, you get to school before dawn every day and arrive home after dinner. It feels like it's been an ice age since you last saw any light, and it's getting you down.

What to Do About It

Get sunshine and natural light any way you can. First thing in the morning, fling those curtains open. Even if all you see is gray or a sunrise, a little light is better than none. Take walks outside, even if it is cold. And, when all else fails, follow your cat's lead and curl up in the pool of light by the windowsill.

Why It Works

In fall and winter, some people feel more tired and worn down from the decrease in natural light. There's even a name for this condition when it's more severe: seasonal affected disorder (SAD). Doctors and scientists don't yet fully understand what chemically brings on this condition, but they do believe that getting more natural light can make a big difference in your mood.

47

Feet Dragging? Water Works

What's Going On

You're beat, but the day's only half over. You slept like a baby last night, but you can barely muster the energy to get through class, never mind practice and homework after school. When something's just not clicking and you're feeling like a slug, you may not be getting enough water.

What to Do

Drink at least six to eight cups of water every day to keep your bod in working order. If this sounds impossible, remember you don't have to chug half a gallon in one go. Have a glass of water with each meal, and a couple in between. To help keep you drinking, add a little natural flavor. Try a few drops of juice from an orange or a slice of lemon to add zest.

Why It Works

Here's a scary thought: Dehydration can shrink your brain. Besides that, every chemical reaction in your body needs water to work. Going through an average day, you'll lose 10 cups of water—and that's without working up a sweat at the gym. You need to replace that missing H_2O to stay on top of your game, even if your game is checkers.

Make Peace With Perfectionism

What's Going On

At basketball practice last night you finished your sprints third, even though you usually finish first. Then when it came time for drills, you kept tripping over your own feet. Why bother hitting the court tonight when you know you'll only get beaten?

What to Do About It

If perfectionism has you stuck in a funk, focus on feeling proud of your accomplishments instead of obsessing over how you could have done better. Remember that excellence comes from lots of practice and small improvements, not by instant perfection. When you start to tell yourself you should have made five baskets in the game instead of just four, stop and figure out the positive spin: Those eight points you did get weren't chump change.

Why It Works

When you're pushing yourself to be your best, positive thinking will get you there a lot faster than negative criticism. Plus, you'll never achieve your goals if you give up because you can't do something perfectly.

Loosen Up

Has stress got a grip on your jaw? Try this stretch for relaxing those gritting teeth:

1. Place the tips of your index fingers on your jaw joints, just in front of your ears.

2. Clench your teeth and take a deep breath through your nose.

3. Count to three, and then exhale, saying "Ahhhhhh" and unclenching your teeth.

4. Repeat a few times.

Contracting and releasing a muscle relaxes it—just the thing for your jaw muscles if stress has been overworking them.

No More Test Stress

What's Going On

The chemistry final is coming up fast. You're trying to study, but this is your worst subject ever. You can't even think about failing this test. But you can't think about anything else either.

What to Do About It

You'll never pass if you don't think you will. Visualization can help you overcome your fears and cynicism. Try this:

1. Sit at a desk or table with a piece of paper in front of you.

2. Close your eyes and imagine you're in the room where you'll be taking the test.

3. Picture your teacher passing out the tests and handing one to you.

4. Now, take a deep breath or two and imagine starting the test. Think about how the questions look on the sheet.

5. See yourself answering them confidently.

Why It Works

Imagining yourself doing well is the first step to formulating a plan for real success. Plus, terror over a test or an assignment can take more energy than studying or doing the work. Taking the time to relax and remember that you can get through it yanks you out of the head spin and helps you refocus your energy where it's useful.

Sound Advice for Studying

What's Going On

Your brother is blasting the TV in the other room, and you can't concentrate on the two massive tests you are trying to study for.

What to Do About It

Turn to your trusty MP3 or CD player to eliminate distracting sounds. For some people, that might mean rocking out to fast-paced music while cranking through study guides. For those who get distracted by music, downloading white noise or ocean wave sounds or shutting out all sound with noise-canceling headphones will do the trick.

Why It Works

Recent studies have focused on how your body and brain react to different types of sound. For some people, strong beats can stimulate brain waves to resonate in sync with the rhythm. This means that faster tempos can help with concentration and alert thinking. Slow, soothing tunes can affect your study session in different ways, from slowing your heart rate to ramping up your endorphins and lowering your stress hormones. And for those who work best in silence, music can provide a calming, restorative 10-minute study break.

Get Steamy

When overloaded, it's important to take some time out to rejuvenate. A steam facial is a great way to start. You'll need a bath towel, a large mixing bowl that's heat safe (glass or ceramic, not plastic), and lavender oil or dried lavender. Then, follow these instructions.

1. Set the bowl on the kitchen table or countertop and fill it halfway with boiling water. (Be careful—burning yourself is the *opposite* of relaxing.)

2. Add 5–7 drops of lavender oil or a handful of dried lavender.

3. Drape the towel over your head and lean over the bowl, breathing slowly as the steam circles around your face.

4. Stay put for 8–10 minutes—if it gets too hot under there, you can lift a corner of the towel to let in some cool air.

In addition to having soothing aromatherapy benefits, the steam facial does wonders for your skin as it works to pull dirt and oil out of your pores.

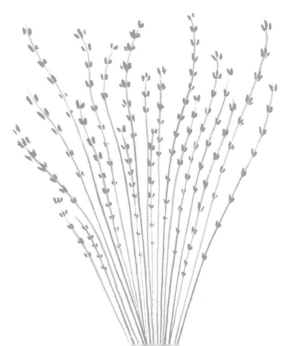

Lose Your Lethargy

What's Going On

Your parents tell you all the time that you're too young to feel tired, but you know the truth. Between schoolwork, sports, and part-time jobs, you're totally burned-out. Dinner time? Does that mean getting up and walking to the kitchen?

What to Do About It

When you're lacking energy and all you want to do is veg, it's time to make way for play. You may not be a kid anymore, but that doesn't mean you have to be *all* business *all* the time. Tap into your inner Rembrandt by painting a picture or working on a scrapbook. Challenge your best pal to a fierce round of Scrabble. Or tackle a jigsaw puzzle or Sudoku.

Why It Works

Games and puzzles stimulate your mind, which can bump up your energy level. They also trick you into thinking about something other than all the stressful things in your life. After a nice play break, you'll be refreshed and able to deal with your commitments with a stronger, relaxed mind.

Punch Out Anger

What's Going On

Society tells you that girls are not supposed to fight, but you've had a helluva day and if you don't hit something—or someone—soon, you're going to explode.

What to Do About It

Don't hurt yourself—or your little brother. Instead, take out your anxiety in a martial arts class like kickboxing or judo. If you can't find a class in your neighborhood or price range, hit the video store. With hundreds of DVDs to choose from, you can turn your room or living room into a training studio in seconds. Just watch out for the lamp when you practice those round kicks.

Why It Works

High-energy forms of exercise like certain types of martial arts offer up a great way to work through anger and other negative emotions. Since they focus on mental discipline as well as physical fitness, martial arts also demand a lot of concentration, which forces you to take your mind off your troubles for a while.

Catch Some Zen

Buddhist meditation is centered around the idea of concentrating on the breath. While everything else around you is always changing, your breath is one thing that remains constant. To try it, just close your eyes and take a few slow, deep breaths. Focus on your inhales and your exhales. Try not to think about anything except breathing. You can also try this exercise by concentrating on your heartbeat. You'll soon notice that having a constant, single point of focus for a few minutes will quiet the mind and stop that crazy chatter in your head.

Order for the Overextended

What's Going On

You have a paper on Japan due on Tuesday, a health quiz on Thursday, a science fair project that has to be ready on Wednesday ... or was the Japan paper for Wednesday? And what day is today, anyway?

What to Do About It

Make a list. It may sound simple, but it really works. Write down everything you need to do and when each thing is due, no matter how big or small. Once you've got everything down, look for small things that you can do right now, go do them, and then cross them off your list. (Yay!) Then scan the list again to decide which of the things left over need to be done first and which can wait for later. Break down big projects into lists of smaller, less intimidating steps.

Why It Works

On paper, things look more doable and less overwhelming. By writing down your assignments, you can lay out in front of you everything that needs to be done—and start doing it. As you check things off the list you'll be able to see where you are and plan what to do next.

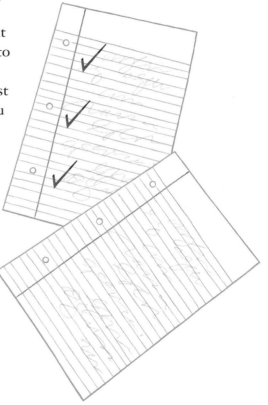

Calmness via Less Caffeine

What's Going On

Finals week has struck. You're tempted to reach for yet another soda while memorizing all the verb tenses in French.

What to Do About It

The occasional cup of coffee, tea, or soda isn't so bad, but be careful about ramping up how much you drink. Doctors suggest keeping caffeine down to 100 milligrams a day—that's about two cans of soda.

Why It Works

Caffeine seems like a quick fix for a bad night's sleep, but after the initial energy jolt (which comes from a short burst of adrenaline) you also get an extra wave of stress hormones, which leads to jitters. This is all followed by a bout of extra low energy when the adrenaline wears off. That's probably way more than you bargained for. Keep an eye on what you're drinking, and you'll keep those shaky hands in check.

Ac-you-pressure

Bet you didn't know that you could do acupressure
on yourself. An ancient but still used Asian healing art,
acupressure follows the idea that pressing on key spots on
the body directly affects other, more distant parts that are
on the same meridian, or energy channel. Want to give it a try?
All you need is 20 minutes and a couple of tennis balls.

Put the two tennis balls in a sock and tie the end. Then, lie
down on your back and put the sock under your neck so
the balls are pressed against the base of your skull.

The edge where your skull meets your spine
is called the occipital ridge, and it has
two acupressure points

that, according to acupressure theory, tell your whole body to relax. Lying on the tennis balls for 20 minutes will leave your neck and body feeling loose and free.

Sooth Eye Strain

What's Going On

Spending a rainy Sunday afternoon emailing your friends was fun. But now your eyes are wiped out and you have to get going on a paper that's due tomorrow.

What to Do About It

Try these eye-refreshing exercises.

1. Turn away from your computer screen, sit up straight, and close your eyes. Place the palms of your hands over your eyes, giving you a good moment of darkness and warming your peeps.

2. Put your hands down and blink repeatedly, until your eyes are moist.

3. Focus on something far away from you and count to 25. Try to hold your gaze for the whole count, then blink rapidly several times afterward.

4. Next, focus on something nearby while you count to 15. Keep a steady focus on this object for the whole count, then blink rapidly several more times afterward.

5. Keep your head straight and exhale while you roll your eyes upward. Hold them there for a few seconds, then return them to the center while you inhale. Now, repeat the process for each of these directions:

- Down
- Right
- Left
- Upper right corner
- Upper left corner
- Lower right corner
- Lower left corner

Why It Works

The muscles that move your eyes work like other muscles in your body—staring at a screen for hours on end is the equivalent of holding out a dumbbell with no break. Focusing at different distances and looking in different directions gives your eye muscles a chance to relax before you get sucked back into your computer.

Dance Out Your Stress

What's Going On

You've been working 24/7 on a term paper about *The Odyssey*. Now you're thinking in Greek and your body feels all bound up.

What to Do About It

Crank up the tunes and dance it all out. If structured dance classes are more your style, you can find all sorts of offerings out there, from ballet to hip-hop to hula.

Why It Works

When you put your concentration into dance, whether it's a free-form energy release or an organized lesson, it acts as a moving meditation, giving your mind a chance to be calm. A good jam will take you from Circe, the sea witch, back to your usual goddess self.

Follow Your Nose

To relax your olfactory senses (and the rest of your body),
try a little aromatherapy. You don't need to head to the spa
to do this. Simply place a small amount of rock salt or sea
salt in a small vial or plastic bag. Add a couple of drops of
essential oil to the salt. Some calming ones that can be found
at most health stores are chamomile, rose, lavender, lemon
balm, neroli, and palmarosa. Whenever you feel stressed,
take a whiff. Herbalists say that the scent of an essential oil
activates and soothes the part of your brain that controls
emotion and memory, which is a part of your brain that
also tends to be on edge when you are stressed out.
Ahhhh.

Ditch Your Insomnia

What's Going On

You tried counting sheep, and when that didn't work, you branched off into goats and pigs. Now, it's three hours before you have to get up, and you're still wide awake.

What to Do About It

You need a sleep ritual—a pattern you fall into every night before you go to bed. Try drinking caffeine-free herbal tea, turning down the lights and meditating, or reading something mellow for 15 minutes. (Don't include TV or surfing the Internet in the mix—those things will only stimulate you.) Practice the same routine every night before you go to bed.

Why It Works

Your body responds to cues that it's time to slow down and sleep. Many people already respond to darkness by feeling sleepy, but if you don't, you can teach your body new cues by repeating these mellow activities just before going to bed. After a while your body will associate your bedtime routine with being tired.

Drink Tea for Zzzs

What's Going On

You don't usually have trouble falling asleep, but if you exercise too late in the day or drink one too many cans of Coke, you sometimes feel too wired to go to bed.

What to Do About It

Sleep is important. You can calm your nervous system with a cup of caffeine-free chamomile tea. It's easy to do: Just steep a bag in boiling water for 10 minutes, sit back, and enjoy.

Why It Works

Many scientists and herbologists believe that chamomile, a flower that looks like a daisy but tastes very different, acts on the same part of the brain as anti-anxiety drugs, allowing you to relax and get ready for bed. It also soothes upset stomachs, which sometimes occur when you're wired and stressed.

Get Loopy

Knitting and crochet aren't just
for grannies anymore. If you're
looking for a fun way to chill
out, think about working
with yarn. You can knit or
crochet with friends (groups
are popping up everywhere)
or pack projects with you. The
repetition of the act of stitching
causes your mind to be single-
focused, which is what meditation is about.
And an extra bonus: This form of meditation
generates new scarves and sweaters.

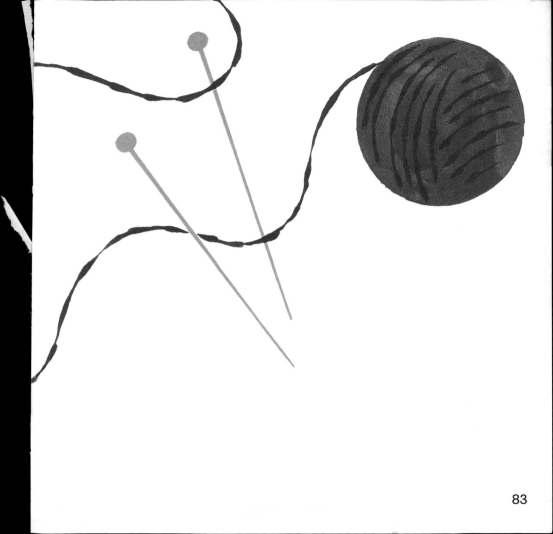

83

Exhale Your Exasperation

What's Going On

Ever get too mad to think straight? Your blood pressure rises and your head suddenly feels all weird and confused? You're probably not getting enough air.

What to Do About It

You can begin to diffuse your anger by getting your breathing back to normal. Try this:

1. Put your hand on your belly, just below your belly button.

2. Breathe in slowly through your nose, watching your hand move as your belly expands.

3. Hold your breath and count to three.

4. Breathe out slowly through your mouth.

5. Repeat steps 1 to 4 several times.

Why It Works

When you're stressed out, your breathing tenses up and you don't get enough air into your body. Not getting enough oxygen stresses out your body even more. Deep breaths bring in that oxygen, helping you relax and think.

Just Say No

What's Going On

You'd do anything for your friends. And they know that. So you are always doing EVERYTHING for your friends. How do you decide where to draw the line?

What to Do About It

You have to learn how to set priorities, and when to say no. It's a crucial skill, especially when you're already maxed out. Before you take on a new responsibility, ask yourself these questions:

- Do I have to do this, or could someone else do it?

- Does it need to be done at all?

- What's the worst thing that would happen if I didn't do this?

- Then, compare the urgency of the task with something else competing for its time. If only one can get done, which one is more important?

Why It Works

If you let yourself get pulled in 50 directions at once, everything can start to feel like it's out of control. And once you've lost a grip on what you're doing and why, you're headed for some serious stress. To stay in control, set priorities and stick to them, keeping in mind that you are not being selfish when you sometimes say "no"—you are just staying sane.

Feel-Good Foot Soak

A day of pounding the pavement in search of a summer job has left you with aching feet and frayed nerves. Tackle both with this foot treatment.

1. In a small bowl, combine 2 tablespoons table salt, 2 tablespoons olive oil, and 2 tablespoons liquid hand soap to make a scrub. Mix them well.

2. Fill a big bowl with warm water and 2 or 3 drops of eucalyptus or peppermint oil.

3. Soak your feet in the big bowl while you add a couple of splashes of water to the scrub mixture—just enough to build up a lather.

4. Pull your feet out of the water, massage the scrub into them, and let them sit for a couple of minutes before returning to the water.

5. Soak for a few more minutes and rinse. Your feet—and your mind—will be ready again for action.

Fresh Cure for Headaches

What's Going On

Your parents are on your case—again. Your mom's been yelling all day, and at this point you're no longer sure why. Now your head is throbbing.

What to Do About It

Headaches are no fun, but there are ways to get rid of them. Most people take the usual pharmaceuticals, but why don't you try something more natural? Peppermint can be great for tension-type headaches. To try it, just dab a little peppermint oil on your forehead and temples, breathe deeply, and let it work its minty magic.

Why It Works

Mint is said to improve blood flow around the forehead, and its strong scent will help clear away the thoughts that have given you the headache in the first place.

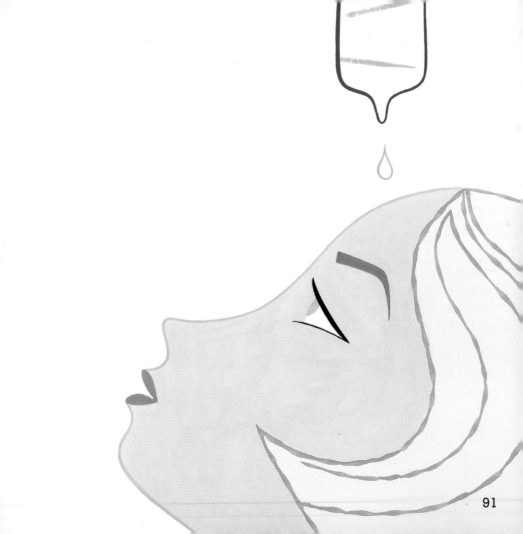

Ramped Up? Veg Out

What's Going On

Everything is getting to you lately. Even your four-legged friend has been at the receiving end of some four-letter words.

What to Do About It

Your diet matters. If every little thing is sending you over the edge, you might not be getting the stress-fighting nutrients you need. Every day you need at least five portions of fruit and vegetables. According to the USDA, a portion is about $1/2$ cup (or 4 ounces), equal to one small apple, two plums, or half a cup of mixed vegetables.

Why It Works

Your body chemistry depends a lot on what you eat. In order to make serotonin, the feel-good chemical, your brain needs a steady supply of nutrients like vitamin B6, found in foods like potatoes, bananas, and garbanzo beans. Folic acid, along with vitamins B3 and B12, are also useful in fighting stress. You'll find these nutrients in leafy green vegetables, nuts, fish, and fortified cereals. It's also good to stay away from things that cause stress, like too much caffeine and sugar.

Curl Up in a Ball

What's Going On

Period cramps, insensitive boys, nightmare teachers. Sometimes you just want to lie down and curl up in a ball.

What to Do About It

Fortunately, the ancient yogis felt the same way. One of the most basic poses from yoga, Child's Pose (or Balasana in Sanskrit), is a curled-up position that's all about getting yourself back to a calm frame of mind. Follow these steps:

1. Kneel on the floor, with your knees apart so they're right under your hips.

2. Bring your feet together and sit on your heels.

3. Lean forward, stretching your back as you bring your head to the floor. You can stretch your arms in front of you, with palms down, or lay them at your side with palms up.

4. Stay in this position for at least 30 seconds, or for a few minutes if you like, concentrating on your breathing.

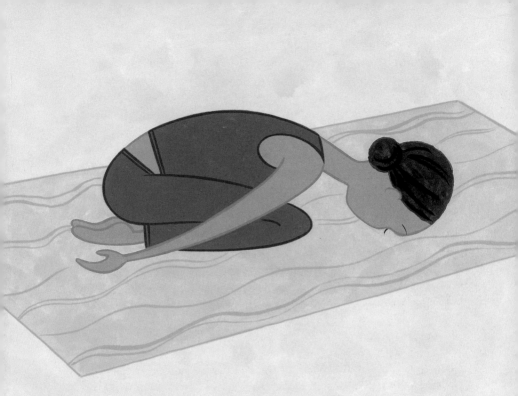

Why It Works

This pose gently stretches your hips, back, and ankles—and keeping your forehead pressed to the floor (with your forehead skin pulling down) allows your brain to calm down and relax.

About the Contributors

Tanya Napier is a writer, designer, and art director. Her work has been published in Boston, New York, and San Francisco. She is also the author and designer of *The Totally TEA-riffic Tea Party Book*. Tanya grew up in England, graduated from Brown University, and now resides in San Francisco.

Jen Kollmer is a San Francisco-based freelance writer, a filmmaker, and a former engineer. Her dramatic works have been published in *Fourteen Hills* journal and staged at the Kennedy Center and in the Marin Headlands. She also coauthored Zest Books' *Girl in a Fix: Quick Beauty Solutions (and why they work)*.

Ali Douglass is a San Francisco-based freelance illustrator. Her work has been featured in advertisements, greeting cards, and apparel, and in publications such as *The NY Times*, *YM*, and *Seventeen*.